MW00718506

YOUR TICKET TO A BETTER TICKET

A Fan's Guide For The Best Concert Experience

By
Steven G. Maples

Edited By
Erin Hand

Copyright 1996
By Steven G. Maples

All rights reserved. No part of this book may be
reproduced, in any form or by any means, without
permission in writing from the publisher.

ISBN 0-9653448-2-7

Printed in USA

Acknowledgments

I dedicate this book to my children, Steven Craig Maples, Stefany Christine Maples; my father, Al Maples; and my mother, Shirley Maples.

I could not have written this book without the support and motivation of these people. A very special thanks to Mark Cowherd at Vision Four Publications who often gave me the confidence and inspiration to complete this book. A special thanks to the following people for helping me to fulfill a dream.

Mark Cowherd   Tom Estes
Joey Dennis   Chuck Clark
Deborah Weems   Mike Vojticek
Kimberly Behl   Christy Martin
Carolyn Maples   Sherry Stiglets
Donna Dean   Ken Mason

TABLE OF CONTENTS

Introduction

This book was written for anyone who would like to know more about concerts and how the behind-the-scenes concert environment works. This book will provide you with some valuable information that will show you how to buy the best seats, how to locate and find the premium parking places, how to avoid the long lines at the concession stand and restrooms, how to meet your favorite entertainer, and, most importantly, how to have fun in a safe environment. Furthermore, this book contains chapter highlights and a glossary of terms to assist the reader with some of the topics discussed in this book.

The book offers several suggestions to concert-goers for enhancing your concert experience. We will explore a typical venue and how it functions. As we explore the venue, we will review the basic operations of the venue as it relates to the concert-goer. Some common and simple methods for communicating with the concert-goer will also be reviewed. After reading this book, you will have a better understanding of the concert environment and how the concert system functions. If you take the time to read this book and follow up on the information this book provides for you, I can guarantee that your concert experience will be much more enjoyable the next time. Even if you have never attended concerts, but have children who do, then this book will provide you with some valuable and not commonly known information. I think it's time for you, the fan, the person paying for the ticket and the concerned parents, to have a better understanding of just what concerts are all about.

In most cases, I can only give you general information as it pertains to concerts and the venues at which these concerts take place. The reason for this is because it will depend on the city, county, state, artist, promoter, and, most importantly, the venue as it relates to the Do's & Don'ts. The rules and regulations that govern these venues will vary accordingly.

The Do's & the Don'ts I will share with you will help you to make your concert experience much more enjoyable. If you follow some of the recommended guidelines and Do's and Don'ts stated in this book, you will enhance your concert experience.

I have been in this type of work for approximately twenty years, and I very much enjoy the music and entertainment that all of us are so fortunate to have. I have attended or worked over 200 different concerts. The concert environment should and can be a very rewarding and positive experience. I firmly support live concerts and remain optimistic that they will continue for many years to come. I would like to share with you some tips for having fun in as safe an environment as possible where you particularly have to deal with immense crowds. I hope you will enjoy reading this book and that you, the patron, fan, and parent, will feel much more comfortable the next time you or someone you know decides to attend a concert.

Concert Experience

38 Special
Aaron Tippin
Aerosmith
Air Supply
Alabama
Alan Jackson
All-4-One
Amy Grant
Bad Company
Barbara Mandrell
Barry Manilow
BB King
Beach Boys
Bill Cosby
Billy Dean
Billy Joe Royal
Billy Ray Cyrus
BJ. Thomas
Bob Hope
Bon Jovi
Bonnie Raitt
Boston
Boyz 11 Men
Cameo
Captain & Tennille
Charlie Daniels
Charlie Pride
Charlie Rich
Chet Atkins
Chicago
Commodores
Conway Twitty
Dan Fogelberg
Daryle Singletary

David Lee Roth
Def Leppard
Dolly Parton
Don Williams
Doobie Brothers
Dottie West
Dr. Hook
Dwight Yoakam
Eagles
Earl Thomas Conley
Earth Wind & Fire
Foghat
Foreigner
Frankie Valli
Gap Band
Garth Brooks
Gary Morris
George Jones
Glen Campbell
Hall & Oates
Hank Williams Jr.
Heart
Helen Cornelius
Holly Dunn
Huey Lewis
Isley Brothers
Jeff Foxworthy
Jethro Tull
Jim Ed Brown
Jimmy Buffett
John Cougar
John Denver
John Snyder
Johnny Cash

Juice Newton
Kansas
Ken Mellons
Kenny Rogers
Kiss
Kris Kristofferson
Larry Gatlin
Lee Greenwood
Leo Sayer
Leon Russell
Lionel Richie
Little Richard
Little River Band
Loretta Lynn
Lori Morgan
Loverboy
Lynyrd Skynyrd
Marshall Tucker Band
Marty Robbins
Mary Chapin Carpenter
Mel Tillis
Melissa Manchester
Merle Haggard
Metallica
Michael Bolton
Michelle Wright
Moody Blues
Motley Crue
New Edition
O'Jays
Oak Ridge Boys
Olivia Newton John
Pam Tillis
Pat Boone
Patty Loveless
Percy Sledge

Poison
Prince
Pure Prarie League
Quiet Riot
Ralph Emery
Randy Travis
Reba McEntire
Restless Heart
Richard Marx
Rick James
Rick Springfield
Ricky Skaggs
Ringo Starr
Rod Stewart
Ronnie Milsap
Roy Clark
Rush
Sammy Kershaw
Sandi Patti
Sawyer Brown
Scorpions
Seals & Croft
Shenandoah
Statler Brothers
Steve Miller Band
Steven Curtis Chapman
T. Graham Brown
Tammy Wynette
Tanya Tucker
Ted Nugent
The Allman Brothers
The Jacksons
The Judds
The Osmonds
The Pointer Sisters
Three Dog Night

Tina Turner
Tom Jones
Tom T. Hall
Tom Wopat
Tony Orlando & Dawn
Tracy Lawrence
Van Halen
Vince Gill
Waylon Jennings
Whitesnake
Willie Nelson
Yes
ZZ Top

Big Spring Jam
City Stages
Country Music Awards
June Jam
Summer Lights

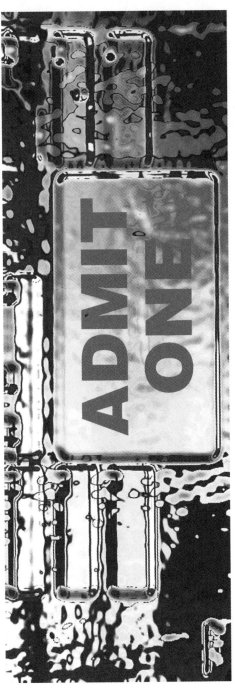

Getting
To
Know
The
Venue

Get to know your venue, arena, amphitheater, or whatever you want to call it. If your venue is city, county, or state-owned, it was probably your tax dollar that paid for it. Venues that fall into this category are most often also operated by the city, county, or state. The venue Manager will typically report to a governing agency such as a Board of Directors or to a City Manager. Other venues may be government-owned, but still contracted out to other parties, called Private Management, to be operated and maintained. This type of arrangement with a Private Management firm appears to be growing; however, most venues are not under a Private Management contract.

If you particularly want to get to know your venue, and you really want to have an enjoyable concert experience, then start by obtaining the following fundamental information from the venue. Keep this information handy so that when you need it, you will have it. You may want to attach this information to the front of your refrigerator.

CONCERT INFORMATION

- Name of Venue
- Name and Phone Number of Venue Manager
- Name and Phone Number of Box Office Manager
- Name and Phone Number of Security Manager
- Mailing Address
- Primary Telephone Number
- Direct Line Phone Number For Purchasing Tickets
- Ticket Information Phone Line
- Business Hours
- Box Office Hours
- Special Important Notes

Now that you have obtained the very basic and fundamental information that virtually every other concert-goer in the world has, it's time to start collecting some extremely valuable information that very few people have. With this information, you will be several steps ahead of the average person that attends concerts. Getting this information is the first step in broadening your knowledge of the concert environment. I will guarantee you that just this information alone will provide you with a better opportunity to buy the best seats in the venue. Your concert experience will be so much more enjoyable because you will feel like a part of the show.

YOUR TICKET TO A BETTER TICKET

The venue's **Mission Statement** will be of great value to you. It should give you a very good indication of what to expect as a ticket buying customer. The mission statement should reflect the goals of the organization.

Direct-In Dialing will speed up the time that it would ordinarily take if you are calling the main phone number and then being transferred by an phone operator or an automated attendant.

Management's direct-in dial phone number will take you directly to a person that can get things done. If you do not want to waste time and think that you have a serious problem, don't hesitate to call management. If you are unable to reach the Manager, his or her administrative assistant or someone in upper management will more than likely call you back. By this time, you have already received some attention.

Please keep in mind that you will not need to call the venue Manager for every detail, and, in most cases, there are several other employees in most organizations who can solve the majority of the problems you may experience as a concert-goer. However, it's sure nice to have access to this office.

Seating Charts are extremely important, and I would strongly encourage you to obtain one and keep it at home and near your phone. You will need to take the time to familiarize yourself with the seating chart. The very first thing you should do is mark your North, South, East and West directions onto the chart. This will help you to maintain some sense of direction for getting around in the venue. You will learn to make some very important notes on this seating chart. I doubt very seriously if this chart will have a scale or be of any value for actual measurements; however, I would definitely recommend you visit the venue and make notes on the seating chart.

Venue Diagrams are not to be confused with seating charts. A venue diagram will have much more detail than a typical seating chart. The venue diagram may have a scale and should indicate the location of entrances, exits, restrooms, concession stands, and telephones, as well as a few other significant attributes of a venue. You may have to request a venue diagram from the venue administration. If you are able to obtain a venue diagram, I would suggest you attach it to your seating chart. It will take both the seating chart and the venue diagram to help determine the best seats for your concert experience. I will give you several different tips for selecting the best seats and how to buy those seats in the next few chapters.

The following two charts illustrate the difference between a typical seating chart and a typical venue diagram.

SEATING CHART

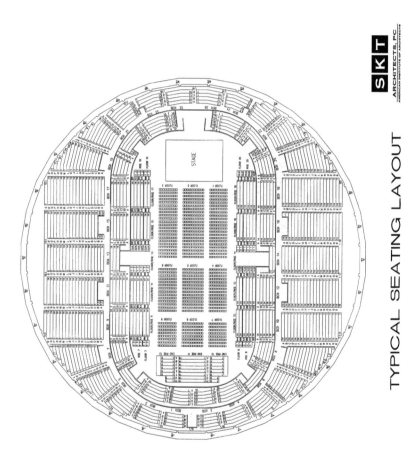

VENUE DIAGRAM

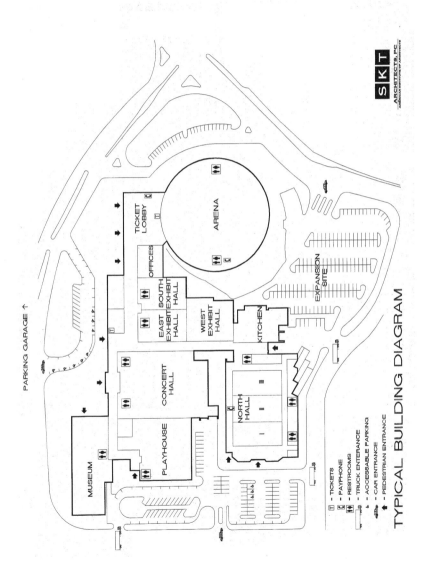

TYPICAL BUILDING DIAGRAM

PARKING GARAGE ↑

ARENA

TICKET LOBBY

OFFICES

EAST EXHIBIT HALL

SOUTH EXHIBIT HALL

WEST EXHIBIT HALL

KITCHEN

EXPANSION SITE

CONCERT HALL

NORTH HALL

PLAYHOUSE

MUSEUM

- TICKETS
- PAYPHONE
- RESTROOMS
- TRUCK ENTERANCE
- ACCESSABLE PARKING
- CAR ENTRANCE
- PEDESTRIAN ENTRANCE

SKT
ARCHITECTS, PC
AMERICAN INSTITUTE OF ARCHITECTS

Group Sales ticket information can be of great value to you for numerous reasons. It's possible that if you can qualify for a group sale, you might acquire a discount on your ticket price. To qualify for the group sale price, you will typically be required to purchase a minimum number of tickets. Keep in mind that the minimum number of tickets

Good
Resources
Offer
U
Premium
Seats
And
Less
Expensive
Seats

will vary accordingly with each venue and act. You may also want to check into group ticket sales as it relates to seating location. Ordinarily, group sales tickets are spread throughout the seating area; however, you may do better with group sales than standing in line for several hours. You may be able to purchase tickets through group sales even when the concert is expected to sell out. The more often you purchase tickets through group sales, the better your seat locations will be. Keep group sales in mind the next time a big name concert artist or group plays your area. A few friends can get together and place one order with the group sales office. Do not wait until tickets go on sale and then go to the box office for these tickets; for group sales to be effective, you should contact the venue as soon as possible.

Mailing Lists will provide you with information about upcoming event activities. Mailing lists are sometimes free to you, the customer; however, some venues do charge a small fee for this service. I would strongly recommend that you call or write any venue that you might visit and request to be added to their mailing list. Sometimes this will give you a little more time to plan and budget for upcoming concerts. If the timing is right, you will hear about upcoming concerts *prior to any official announcements*. How many times have you heard about a concert that is already on sale, and you didn't even know about it? I hear this all the time from some of our regular concert-goers. Sometimes the promoter tries to get by with a cheap advertising budget. In most cases this is not a good idea.

A **Concert Agenda** will help you better track and plan your restroom and concession breaks. This is one way to avoid those long lines. This concert agenda is not readily available to the public, but it is possible to get one. I would start by requesting one from the venue management. If you can talk to the right person, all

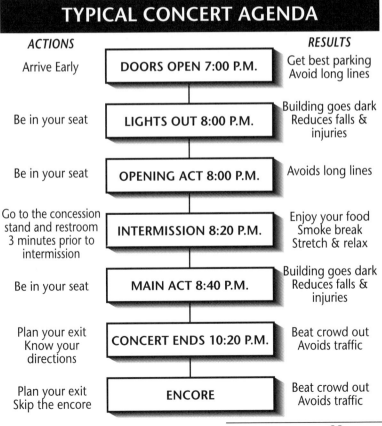

TYPICAL CONCERT AGENDA

ACTIONS		RESULTS
Arrive Early	**DOORS OPEN 7:00 P.M.**	Get best parking Avoid long lines
Be in your seat	**LIGHTS OUT 8:00 P.M.**	Building goes dark Reduces falls & injuries
Be in your seat	**OPENING ACT 8:00 P.M.**	Avoids long lines
Go to the concession stand and restroom 3 minutes prior to intermission	**INTERMISSION 8:20 P.M.**	Enjoy your food Smoke break Stretch & relax
Be in your seat	**MAIN ACT 8:40 P.M.**	Building goes dark Reduces falls & injuries
Plan your exit Know your directions	**CONCERT ENDS 10:20 P.M.**	Beat crowd out Avoids traffic
Plan your exit Skip the encore	**ENCORE**	Beat crowd out Avoids traffic

they really need to do is go backstage and copy it right off the Production Manager's office door. If you cannot obtain one, plan a restroom and concession break approximately 20 minutes after the opening act starts.

Business Hours are easy to obtain. All you need to do is call the venue and request this information. However, the box office hours may be different, so be sure to ask what the box office hours are. Some venues will keep the box office open a few minutes later than the business hours. This might be done for customer service reasons and to help deal with all those late ticket buyers.

Typically, the **doors** for a concert will **open** one hour to one & one half hours prior to the concert. If you are attending a reserved seat show, people usually will not come early unless there is a problem with parking. However, if you are attending a GA (general admission) show, people will normally come early to have a better chance of acquiring the best seat locations. Not many people come early to eat; however, I think that is slowly changing now that more venues are providing name brand type foods.

Camera Policies will definitely vary from one concert to the next. For the most part, this will be the decision of the artist or group performing. Most artists will typically allow small (35 millimeter) cameras. In most cases, a video recorder is not allowed inside the venue. I would recommend reading the back of the ticket and/or calling the venue to verify what the policy will be for the concert in question.

Smoking and Non-Smoking issues are a concern for practically every venue in the country. The handling of this issue will vary a great deal from one venue to the next. You have venue policies, city ordinances, and federal regulations to deal with. If you are a non-smoker, then you won't have too much concern with this issue. On the other hand, if you are a smoker, you may want to find out where the designated smoking areas are. If the venue is a smoke-free venue, then you will probably be asked to step outside to light up. It has been my experience that many concert-goers will smoke inside even if it is a smoke-free venue. It's just too difficult for a small event staff to control all the smokers. However, I would strongly encourage all concert-goers to comply with the venue's smoking policies.

Parking Information should be made available to you if requested. Some venues freely publish this information as part of their customer service program. You should be aware that parking is often one of the most difficult obstacles that a concert-goer has to deal with. The cost for parking will vary from one venue to the next. The parking lots that are located closer to the venue may cost more, but I can assure you that in most cases it would probably be money well spent. Look for parking areas that have adequate lighting at night. Try to park near a landmark or something that is easy to remember. Shuttles or other transportation services are sometimes available when parking off site. If you cannot locate parking on site, I would recommend the nearest controlled and secured parking garage. We sometimes forget about safety concerns and try to save a few dollars and park in empty and non-secured parking lots. If parking is a problem or concern, I would call the venue for recommendations. When possible, walk to and from the venue in groups. Safety should always be taken into consideration when searching for a parking space.

Disability Concerns should be and need to be addressed with the venue. If you have any concerns, I would recommend that you contact the venue. If you would just let the venue know of your disability concerns before you arrive, you will find things go so much smoother. Most venues are required to comply with the Americans with Disabilities Act and, therefore, should be making the necessary modifications that would allow the disabled fair and reasonable access to the venues. The majority of venues have designated seating areas for the disabled, so be sure to inform the venue, if applicable, when purchasing tickets.

Recording your **Seat Locations** prior to leaving home is very important. You should record your exact seat location and leave it with anyone who may have a need to contact you. For example, a baby sitter with this information could reach you faster via the venue if an emergency were to arise. It may be reasonably difficult to get venues to make announcements for several reasons. However, if an emergency call comes in with specific seat locations, then the person can be located.

An **Emergency Phone Number** should be left with someone who might need to contact you in case of an emergency. A pager works great for this use, if you happen to have one. If you do not have a pager, I would definitely let someone know the venue telephone number and your seat location. Some venues have a system in place that would allow you to sign up and record your name and seat location with them. Then, if you receive an emergency phone call, someone will come and get you and, in some cases, even bring you a cellular phone. This is an excellent customer service program, and I would strongly encourage you to take advantage of this program.

Information Packets for concert-goers are available at some venues. These packets may include the Do's & Don'ts that will apply to the venue. Any specific concerns that are not in the information packet should be directed to the venue.

Concession Menus with prices may be available. I would certainly request one so that I would be prepared to order when I get to the concession stand. Again, this will speed up your visit to the concession stand. When reviewing the concessions menu, look carefully for the best buy for the dollar.

Alcoholic Beverages may or may not be sold at the concert. Again, it will depend on a variety of things. Does the venue typically sell alcoholic beverages, what type of crowd is attending, will there be several people under age present, are there sponsorship concerns, and other reasons. You may be required to wear an I.D. wristband if you are going to purchase or consume alcoholic beverages. There may be a limit on how many drinks you can purchase at one time. Alcoholic beverages may be cut off and not sold prior to the concert being over. You will not be able to leave the venue with alcoholic beverages in most cases. If you have observed someone who appears to have consumed an excessive amount of alcohol, then I would encourage you to report your observations to the nearest venue employee. We would all like to have a good time, but let's encourage our concert friends to not drink and drive. Check with your venue for special designated drivers programs.

A **Parents' Room** is a dedicated space where you, the parent, can go and wait for your son, daughter, or friend to return. This really works well in some cases when you may not feel totally comfortable leaving your child. Usually, tables and chairs will be provided, and if you're fortunate and the venue is customer service oriented, they will provide you with soft drinks and snacks. You may want to bring some cards or something to do while you're waiting. By request, you could probably go in to see how things are going if you're concerned. You may take this opportunity to review the content of what your son, daughter, or friend may be listening to.

You should be able to obtain the information about the availability of a parents' room from either guest services, marketing, the box office manager, the telephone operator, and, of course, if all else fails, go directly to the top and call the venue Manager's office.

HIGHLIGHTS

- Obtain direct-line phone numbers for faster connections when ordering tickets.
- Obtain a venue building diagram for recording valuable information.
- Check with Group Sales department for special discounts.
- Be sure to request any free mail outs that the venue may provide when requested.
- Call the venue for video recorders and camera policies.
- Call the venue for the best parking information on the day of the concert.
- Call the venue for any disability concerns.
- Leave your seat location and the venue's phone number with someone in case of an emergency.

Getting
To
Know
The
Staff

ENTERTAINER'S STAFF

An entertainer's staff is the heart and soul of the event and can certainly make or break your concert experience. You may have paid good money to see your favorite entertainer; however, I can assure you that if the staff on either side fails to get their job done and done well, then your concert experience might not be so pleasant. A typical entertainer will travel across the country to perform concerts with a staff of twenty to one hundred people. For the most part, the staff will travel by buses and eighteen-wheelers. It's not uncommon for an entertainer to arrive at a venue with two to eight buses and two to twelve eighteen-foot tractor trailers. It takes this type of storage space to carry around all the equipment that shows are carrying today. It's just unbelievable how much sound and lighting equipment is on those trucks. This staff will usually travel all across the country. They often barely have enough time to get to the next venue, unload the trucks, build the set, hang the lights, hang the sound, and do a ready check prior to the show. At the conclusion of the show, this crew, with the help of the local crews, will have to take it all down and put it all back on the trucks and get ready for the next town. It has been my experience that the average concert will take eight to ten hours to set up once everything has arrived. It will also take another two to eight hours to take it all down and load it back onto the trucks. This crew will work very close with the local crews in order to come together and provide a team effort to accomplish the enormous task before them.

To watch these crews come together and assemble such an overwhelming stage and set is just unbelievable. Sometimes there are hundreds of people working together to make this happen. I find the rigging of events to be the most fascinating and interesting part. To observe riggers climbing a few hundred feet in the air to tie off the sound and lights is definitely a sight to see, and to watch these people walk around on narrow steel I beams is often breathtaking. Without these people, we would not have the opportunity to attend concerts that are staged in such a professional manner. The production crew that travels with an artist will spend a lot of time on the road and will earn every dollar that he or she will make. All of these people are to be commended for helping to make our concert experiences so great.

VENUE STAFF

The venue staff, on the other hand, is the heart and soul of the venue and can certainly make or break your concert experience. I want to take this opportunity to commend all the many different people that work in the concert environment. The following are some typical job titles and responsibilities for those positions. Responsibilities will vary from one venue to the next.

- **President, Vice President, Director, Executive Director, Manager, General Manager** – familiar job titles of the staff person on site and in charge of the venue.

- **Vice President, Assistant Director, Associate Director, Assistant Manager, Director of Operations** – job titles of the second person in charge.
- **Director of Finance, Comptroller** – responsible for all accounting data such as financial statements, invoicing, payroll, concert settlements, human resources, and insurance.
- **Director of Marketing, Marketing Manager, Sales Representative** – responsible for marketing events, booking space, advertising, public relations, group sales
- **Box Office Manager** – responsible for day to day operation of box office. Setup events, record keeping, ticket holds, monies, part time staff assignments
- **Director of Operations, Manager of Operations** – manages departmental budgets, event setup, venues, maintenance, engineering, very much involved with day to day event activity
- **Director of Security, Manager of Security, Public Services Director** –responsible for crowd control management, security, parking, ticket takers, ushers
- **Production Manager** – responsible for technical event related items, stagehands, riggers, sound and lights
- **Engineering Director, Manager** – responsible for venue maintenance, preventative maintenance, utilities, projects, HVAC
- **Event Coordinator** – responsible for coordinating with the lessee and or promoter to work out the details of the event. Distributes information to the venue staff. Serves as primary contact to venue.

- **Concessions Manager** – responsible for the products sold in concessions, large part time staff, novelties, alcoholic beverages
- **Catering Manager** – responsible for backstage catering, alcoholic beverages
- **Bar Manager** – responsible for alcoholic beverages
- **Operations, Event Support** – responsible for event setup, janitorial services, staging, chairs, tables
- **Engineering** – responsible for HVAC, electrical, equipment repairs
- **Security** – responsible for venue security, and crowd control
- **T-Shirt Security** – performs security task in front of the stage and around the mixer platform and special assignments
- **Ticket Takers** – responsible for validating and taking patrons ticket
- **Ushers** – responsible for assisting patrons with seat location
- **Stagehand** – performs task such as loading and unloading trucks
- **Rigger** – works above the stage area tying off the sound and lighting equipment

Event
Awareness

Marketing venues and creating a concert marketing strategy can be a real challenge at times. Of course, if you're going on sale with a big name entertainer, then it's no problem. (Just build it, and they will come.) We wish. The concert market is a very strange environment; you just never know how many people will be there until you count the number of tickets. Marketing an event will vary depending on several different things; however, you will probably first hear about the event via some form of advertising such as radio, cable television, or newspaper. There are other methods of advertising and other ways to find out about concerts, so stay tuned for more information in this area.

Mailing Lists are compiled and usually kept in some database file at the venue. This mailing list is a good source for venues that may want to conduct surveys or just frequently mail you concert information. One good thing about being on the mailing list is that you sometimes find out what's going on at the venue early enough to make plans accordingly. I would strongly encourage you to get on the mailing list. There should not be a charge for this; after all, you are the potential paying customer. To get on the mailing list, you may need to call the venue and provide them with all the necessary information. A mailing list is a great vehicle for communicating with the concert-goer and, of course, is another means of advertising.

Monthly Calendars are provided by many of the venues. This may be a graphic-type calendar, or it just might be in some form of line item type format. This is very good information if you want to stay in touch with what's going on at the venue. This calendar may be included in the mail-out, but will vary at each venue. Some venues have them available, but do not mail them out. In this case, you may need to go to the venue to obtain your copy.

Trade Magazines are another source for information about up-coming concerts. You can also find out more about your favorite entertainer, if you wish to do so. There are several magazines that will give you complete routing tours and the inside scoop on just about every performer in the country. Information is also available concerning ticket prices and attendance figures.

Kiosks are becoming very popular in the concert industry. A kiosk is used for displaying a variety of information, such as directions, current-event data, upcoming concerts, restaurants, transportation, and other miscellaneous information. Some kiosks are computer-generated and even have the capability of selling you a ticket. The advertisement displayed on the kiosks is often used for a revenue source.

A **Radio Station** is an excellent way of promoting concerts. This is often the way most ticket buyers first hear about concerts. Radio Stations will often have contests to win tickets to the concert, sometimes front row seats. Radio Stations have the capability of getting you really excited and looking forward to the event. I have been told a good D.J. is worth a million dollars; however, it was a D.J. that told me that. A special thanks to all the radio stations for playing the music.

The **Newspaper** is also a good way of advertising concerts. Look for the larger concert ads to be in Sunday's paper. Fridays are often good days to look for upcoming concerts, also. The reason for this is that many concerts go on sale on Saturday.

Cable Television is an excellent way of reaching the teenagers that attend concerts. The music industry has continued to increase its popularity with increased television exposure.

The **Internet** is the latest wave of advertisement for the concert market. If you have access to the Internet, you will find that a vast number of venues now have a home page. You will also find that several artists have a home page. The home page will provide you with a tremendous amount of information. The World Wide Web is a remarkable communication tool. If you do not have the Internet address for a particular concert or venue, you can start by searching for concerts. Two popular search engines are WebCrawler and Yahoo. It is very easy to find this information on the Internet.

HIGHLIGHTS

- Event awareness can be an excellent vehicle for improving your seat location.
- Monthly calendars with upcoming event activities are often free of charge and can be mailed to you by the venue.
- Trade magazines are a very good source for upcoming concerts.
- Radio stations often give away good tickets to concerts. All you typically have to do is listen to win.
- The primary radio station advertising the concert will sometimes give away front row seats for the concert.
- Radio stations are often a very good source for concert information.
- Look for the larger concert ads to be in the Sunday newspaper.
- Look for a concert calendar to be printed in the newspaper. The entertainment section is often used for concert advertisements.
- The Internet is an excellent tool for obtaining concert information. It is extremely easy and to your advantage to access concert information on the Internet.

Box
Office

The **Box Office** is often the first point of contact for you, the ticket-buyer. Often, it is at this point in time that you begin to formulate your opinion about the venue. Was the box office employee customer service oriented, and were you given the necessary information to make your decision about what tickets to purchase? This is where it all starts, and, as a ticket-buyer, I would expect to be treated like a customer. Many times, venues lose sight of who the customer is, because of the supply and demand factor. Just because the ticket may be in high demand does not mean that you, the customer, should be treated any differently. So much for customer service in this area of the concert guide.

The Box Office is the designated area in the venue were you can purchase tickets. The location of the box office will vary from one venue to the next. You will find ticket windows on the exterior side of some venues, inside at other venues. I would suspect that very few venues have both. In some cases, the box office might even be adjacent to the venue. It has been my experience that the only things sold at a typical box office are tickets. However, I'm sure that some venues would sell soft drinks at the box office if they thought that would be an additional profit center. Several of the new venues and remodeled older venues have upgraded their box office equipment. You will find faster computers, much improved ticket printers, electronic voice speakers, and video cameras.

If you happen to be an avid concert-goer and you frequently purchase tickets at a specific location, you should develop a friendship with those people. Use this friendship to your advantage. These people can help you with selecting the best seats.

TOP 10 QUALIFICATIONS FOR A GOOD SEAT

1. Reasonably Close View. (Binoculars Not Required)
2. Adequate Leg Room
3. Aisle Seat
4. A Seat Location Where No One Can Stand Up In Front Of You
5. Quick & Easy Access To The Concession Stand
6. Quick & Easy Access To The Restroom
7. Cup Holder
8. Smoking Or Non-Smoking (By Choice)
9. Reasonable Elevation (Not Too Many Steps)
10. Soft & Comfortable Seat

Seating Charts - A seating chart is a graphic display of the venue seating area. These charts are available at the box office and other locations as deemed appropriate by the box office management. Typically, these seating charts are not to any form of scale that would be of any real value to you. However, if the seating chart is scaled, then you could take advantage of this opportunity. I would strongly recommend that you obtain a seating chart that you keep at home. I have observed hundreds of people taking too much time at the box office window selecting a ticket. If the box office has computerized ticketing and other ways to sell, other people are buying good tickets while you are choosing a seat location. You should be prepared prior to walking up to the window, if possible. I know that this is not always possible, but it is highly recommended.

Front Row Seats - Front row seats are exactly that; they are the seats on the first row directly in front of the stage. The distance between the front row and the stage will vary from one venue to another. Sometimes a barricade will be placed in front of the stage for crowd control. The purpose of a barricade is an additional safety measure for everyone involved and is a part of crowd management. A few front row seats may be held for promotional reasons. On occasion, some artists will require that the front row be held and not sold on the first day of sales. The primary reason for this is to keep the ticket scalpers from purchasing the tickets. The artist's designated representative will usually handle the release of these tickets. Sometimes, the designated representative will not sell the tickets, but instead will wait until the evening of the show and select patrons in the upper level to come down and sit on the front row. A radio station will often be issued front row seats for the purpose of promoting the event. To win these tickets, you will need to listen to the radio and possibly compete in some type of contest. The best way to purchase front row tickets is from a ticket outlet that does the least amount of business. You should also keep ticket purchases to a minimum when trying to buy front row seats. An experienced ticket seller will usually have faster key strokes and make less errors when processing a transaction.

How To Purchase Good Seats - There are several ways to purchase good seats. So, for starters, let's make the assumption that you are dealing with a computerized ticketing venue. In other words, all the tickets are being sold via a computerized ticketing system, such as TicketMaster or TicketLink, which I'm somewhat familiar with. Call the venue where the event is taking place and request a list of all ticket locations for this particular event. Make sure you get all the locations and not just the local outlets. In some cases, you can purchase tickets hundreds of miles away from where the event is actually taking place. More often than not, you will find that the outlets located the farthest away from the venue will be a much better choice for purchasing the best tickets. You may have to drive longer, but you won't have to wait as long. If you're lucky, you may even know someone that lives near that unnoticed outlet who can purchase tickets for you. In most cases, you will also have the opportunity to purchase tickets via a phone line, if you are fortunate enough to get through. It is not uncommon to see people standing in line to purchase tickets and also dialing from a cellular phone at the same time. There is that slight chance they may get through on the phone while waiting in line.

If you are familiar with the seating area and know what you want, then the ticket-seller can make a faster transaction which can be very helpful. You may also find that you will sometimes be able to purchase preferred seat locations in smaller quantities starting with two. Some of these computer programmers will have the system skip over two good seats just to find six together. You might find some good seats in odd numbers in rows closer to the stage. The reason for this is because the computer programmer has programmed the system not to leave single seats because they are often hard to sell.

When a concert goes on sale, the venue will be required to hold a certain number of seats for the promoter, artist, radio, sponsor, record labels, sight-line problems (obstructed view), logistics, etc. The venue will more than likely hold some tickets for group sales, relocation, disabled, VIP's, and maybe a few tickets that can be purchased by employees. Most of these holds are legitimate and are required by the promoter and the artist. At some point, typically starting a few days prior to the show, the promoter will start to release these tickets. In some cases, these tickets will not be released until the day of show. The reason for this is that the promoter is unsure of certain speaker locations and or other sight-line problems which may turn out not to be a problem. Sometimes these seats are located just to the side of the stage and may be fairly close. This is one method for possibly purchasing great seats at ticket value. I would encourage you to call the box office starting about three days prior to the show date if you choose to use this method for purchasing tickets. The risk of purchasing tickets late is that you may not get any and run the risk of missing the show.

If you are a member of the fan club of the entertainer for which you are trying to purchase tickets, you may want to call the fan club for special seating. There is fan club seating held for some concerts. Typically, fan club seating on a scale of one to ten and ten being great seats, fan club seating would average out to be a seven – not bad if you did not even have to go down and fight the crowd. This is a great way to buy good seats and even potentially meet your favorite entertainer. See section on Fan Clubs on page 85.

You may also want to check into group sales for special reserved seating. You may be required to purchase a minimum number of tickets to qualify for group sales. Again, group sales seat locations will vary accordingly, but may be as good as six or seven on a scale of one to ten. This is a great way to purchase tickets when applicable, because you can avoid the long lines, since group sales are most often handled over the phone and by mail.

Look and listen for sponsors during the advertisements of concerts. Most of the time these will be name-brand type sponsors, and if you know someone associated with a sponsor, you might be able to purchase some tickets from that sponsor. The radio stations will usually give their tickets away on the air, if they themselves are given any for promotional reasons.

The Internet is moving at a very rapid pace and will offer you several opportunities to purchase tickets in the future. Currently, the Internet is an excellent source for locating concert information, such as tour dates, ticket prices, and phone numbers for ordering tickets.

Backstage Passes are those passes that are required to access the backstage area. The backstage pass is normally a stick-on type pass that you would affix to your clothing. The pass is usually displayed on the chest area or on the leg just slightly above the knee. The pass will be for a specific artist or group and will have a date on it. Several years ago, the backstage pass was much more attainable than it is today. The backstage area and private dressing rooms can be viewed as the home away from home for an artist. Let's not forget that artists need to have some private space just as we all do. A backstage pass does not mean that you will meet your favorite entertainer. It just means you will probably get yelled at by the production crew; if you are not familiar with the backstage area, you will probably get in their way. If you would like to increase your chances of meeting your favorite artist, I would suggest you join his or her fan club. The backstage pass is just not a sure chance of meeting the artist; however, if you want to meet the crew, promoter, production manager, and tour accountant, it might have some value.

Scalped Tickets are those tickets that are being sold at a price higher than face value. Face value is the original selling price that is recorded on the ticket. A person who sells tickets at a cost higher than the original selling price is known as a ticket scalper. There are some people who actually do this for a living. A ticket scalper may even have his or her own business cards, so don't be surprised if you are handed one sometime. Ticket scalping is legal in some states. I believe ticket scalping is a state law if prohibited; however, there may be other local or city laws and venue policies that prohibit ticket scalping. Like any other profession, you have some good and bad ticket scalpers. I suppose that if you're being sold a valid ticket, not being misinformed, and it's legal, then I don't have a problem with it. However, several artists have spoken out against ticket scalpers. I know for sure that some artists are holding front row seats out of the ticket manifest to prevent ticket scalpers from purchasing those tickets. A ticket scalper will typically pay people to spend days in line in an effort to buy the best seats for hot shows. Ticket scalpers will also run ads in the paper advertising great seats for sale; however, they may or may not really be great.

Sometimes you can purchase a good ticket via the newspaper, even at a reasonable price. Some people just need to sell their tickets because something came up, and they have a conflict on a particular date. However, in most cases, the tickets are overpriced.

If you still want a good ticket and have not been able to get one because you did not follow the information I have given you, then you can always try the ticket scalper. However, ticket scalping may or may not be legal in your city. You can check with the local city attorney's office to find out. If you are going to purchase tickets from a ticket scalper, you should do so with caution. You just might be purchasing a counterfeit ticket. Yes, you read this correctly; beware of counterfeit tickets. Furthermore, it would be helpful if you had a venue seating chart when purchasing these tickets. There is a thing called misrepresenting ticket location. The ticket scalper may tell you the seat is in a good location, but what the ticket scalper really meant to tell you is that it is a good hike up to your seat.

Will Call is a designated area at or near the box office for ticket pick up. Will Call tickets are usually phone orders, mail orders, trades, promotional, media, and/or comps that are being picked up on the day of the show. The biggest problem with Will Call tickets is that sometimes the line for these tickets can become very long. Arrive early for will call pick up.

Some venues also have a club you can join with special **Club Seating** which provides some type of first right to purchase tickets prior to sale date. The rules that pertain to this are different from one venue to the next, so you will need to get the details on this from the venue that you support. Be sure to read the fine print if you are going to pay a fee to have the right of first refusal.

A ticket buyer typically will be given several choices for **Method of Payment**. You can certainly pay with cash; however, many ticket-buyers will charge their concert tickets. If you plan to charge tickets, you will need a major credit card such as VISA, MasterCard, Discover, or American Express. You may be required to show a driver's license. If you are going to write a check, also plan on having proper identification. Some venues will not accept checks on the day of show. Call the venue to check on their policies.

More and more concerts are getting **Sponsorship** these days. These sponsors often have a limited number of tickets available to them. If you just happen to know someone associated with a major sponsor, then it may be worth a call to them. Of course, there is always politics and who you know in any type of business.

Finding Your Seat Location does not need to be confusing. You should start by obtaining a seating diagram from the venue or at the point of purchase. Then, very carefully read the ticket for specific location. Look for seat identification, such as level, box number, row, and seat number. The first thing would be to ask the ticket-taker which direction as you pass through the turnstile. Some venues will have their ticket-takers briefly tell you which direction to go as you pass through the turnstile. Don't get bogged down at this point with your exact seating location. Once you get to the general area of your seating, then ask one of the ushers to seat you. I would hope that the usher would ask you, the patron, if you need any assistance locating your seat. Some ushers are just not properly trained for their job, so you may have to ask for help. By the way, I also think that you will typically find that when you are looking directly at the section of seats that you are to be seated in, the seating will start with Seat 1 on the left. If you keep this in mind, then you can avoid having to walk over so many people in those very narrow aisles.

Group Sales is a great way to purchase tickets when applicable. As I stated earlier, group sales tickets will vary and are usually available to anyone when a minimum number of tickets are purchased. You may have to purchase as many as twenty or more tickets to qualify for group sales. You should call the venue where you may be attending concerts for this information. This is usually a pre-order type ticket and is frequently offered to local businesses. If you purchase this ticket, you might even be eligible for a discount. Don't forget to ask. This ticket can be purchased over the phone in most cases. You will be guaranteed tickets even if the event sells out. You can stay home and avoid potential parking problems and long lines. This is a great way to get several friends seating together and have a great time. This is about the only way I know to get a large group of friends all seated together. When most concerts go on sale, they have a limit on how many tickets each person can buy per transaction, unless through group sales.

Tickets

Hard Tickets have their distinct advantages and disadvantages. When I say hard ticket, I'm referring to the fact that I have physical possession of each and every ticket to be sold. Do you remember when you would go to the box office to purchase your tickets, and the ticket seller would tell you what's available, turn to a hard ticket rack and pull off the tickets you wanted to purchase? When using hard tickets, the box office manager would set up a manual seating manifest and order a specific number of tickets from a ticket printing company. This is a manual controlled ticketing system for a box office manager. This meant that if you were the first person in line to purchase tickets, you could be assured that if you wanted front row seats, you could buy them. Some concert-goers may never trust a computerized ticketing system. However, I have spoken with several concert-goers who were opposed to computerized ticketing at first, but now they think it's great. The only real advantage to hard tickets would be that you do not have to depend on the computer to be working in order to purchase tickets. Hard tickets are still around and probably will be for many years to come; however, computerized ticketing is definitely taking over.

There are many common concerns about a computerized system. What about computer hackers; are they finding a way to get into the computer ticketing system and purchasing all those good seats? What about the computer programmers who develop the ticketing software; are they beating the system? I can certainly understand why some concert-goers would not trust the computerized ticketing system. However, I can assure you that a computerized ticketing company will not stay in business very long if these unfair practices were happening.

It has been my experience that most concert-goers have accepted the change in ticket buying and have come to appreciate the computerized ticketing system.

Computerized Tickets have proven to be an excellent way to sell tickets to a concert-goer. Think about it; all the tickets are stored in a computer at some location which may or may not be located in the venue. Several access points have been setup to sell these tickets at a specific time, so the computer will come on and give all concert-goers equal access to all tickets. A typical on-sale date may or may not allow you to purchase tickets at the venue. What I mean by this is that you may have to purchase tickets from a ticket outlet or through a telephone order on the first day. I think this may have something to do with ticketing contracts, surcharges, or some venue policy. At any rate, this may not be the case at the venue you support.

I sometimes use the word "support," because you are the customer and, without you, the venues would close their doors. A computer utilizing many phone lines has the ability to sell hundreds and even thousands of tickets all at the same time. That's why you may be the tenth person in line at some ticket outlet location, but your transaction may be as far back as if you were the one hundredth person in line and probably even much farther back than that. Tickets that are in great demand will go extremely fast on a computerized ticketing system. I'm sure you have heard of record sellouts of thousands of tickets in just a couple of hours.

I think that most venues prefer computerized ticketing, because it has so many positives for the venue, as well as for the ticket buyer. For the venue, it's potentially an additional source of revenue. It also helps keep large crowds away from the venue when tickets go on sale. Most computerized ticketing systems have a very good ticketing control system and are very reliable. In most cases, the customer will have a choice of where to purchase the ticket. This can be a real convenience to you, the customer, because you may not have to drive quite as far just to purchase the ticket, unless you are choosing an out-of-the-way location to get a good seat as described before.

The computerized ticketing systems that I'm familiar with are fair and are definitely in the best interest of the concert-goer. I would prefer to have computerized tickets over hard tickets any day of the week. It has been my experience that most concert-goers are purchasing the better tickets from ticket outlets and not from the venue itself.

The computerized ticketing system offers several advantages to the ticket buyer.

- Equal Access
- Convenience
- More Options
- Phone Access
- Mail Order
- Faster Service
- Additional Points of Purchase
- Improved Customer Service

TYPICAL COMPUTERIZED TICKETING SYSTEM

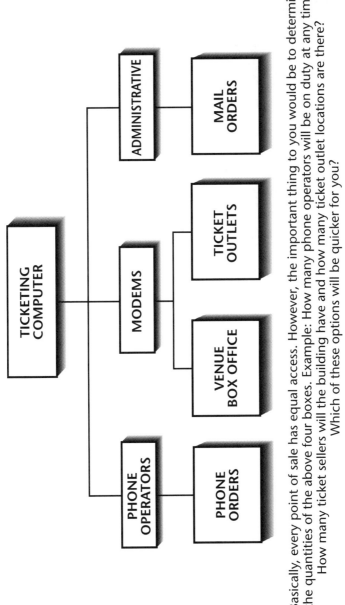

```
                    TICKETING
                    COMPUTER
    ┌──────────────────┼──────────────────┐
PHONE                MODEMS          ADMINISTRATIVE
OPERATORS
    │            ┌──────┴──────┐            │
 PHONE       VENUE          TICKET        MAIL
 ORDERS    BOX OFFICE       OUTLETS      ORDERS
```

Basically, every point of sale has equal access. However, the important thing to you would be to determine the quantities of the above four boxes. Example: How many phone operators will be on duty at any time? How many ticket sellers will the building have and how many ticket outlet locations are there? Which of these options will be quicker for you?

HIGHLIGHTS

- Get to know the ticket sellers. They can assist you with the best seat locations.
- Consider the Top 10 seating qualifications when selecting your seat.
- Obtain a copy of venue seating chart.
- When possible, request a specific seat location for faster service.
- Ticket outlets are most often the best place to purchase the best tickets.
- When trying to purchase front row seats you should keep it to a minimum. You have a better chance of getting front row if you purchase two tickets instead of six tickets, for example.
- Call the venue or ticketing company selling the tickets and request information pertaining to all ticket outlet locations that will be selling tickets for a specific concert.
- The best chance of purchasing front row tickets would be at a ticket outlet that does the least amount of business.
- Look for some good tickets to be released a few days prior to show.
- Consider group sales when purchasing concert tickets.
- To increase your chances of meeting your favorite artists, you should join the fan club.
- Buyer beware when purchasing scalped tickets.
- Computerized ticketing offers many advantages to the ticket buyer.

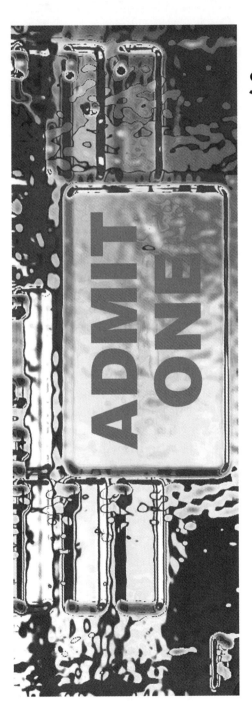

Seating

Reserved Seating is the most widely used method for selling seats to concert-goers. This type of seating will allow you to arrive at the venue early or late and not have to worry about having a good seat when you arrive. However, if you do decide to skip the opening act, don't be surprised if someone is sitting in your seats. Don't panic, and don't go over and attempt to handle the situation yourself. Simply find an usher and show the usher your tickets. Stand back out of the way until the usher has moved the other party, and then gladly take your seats. If, for some reason, the usher does not want to move the people that are in the wrong seats, then request to speak with someone from management. Remember this is a reserved seat show, and you are the ticket holder of a specific seat location. You are entitled to that seat location at any time during the show.

General Admission is exactly that – come as you can and be seated or stand just about anywhere you want to. Of course, you can't stand back stage or in the aisles. In some cases, general admission can be more of a problem than reserved seating. There will always be those concert-goers who arrive twelve hours early so that when the doors open, they can run in and get as close as possible to the stage. Many people try to save seats for all their friends. Then, all of a sudden, everybody shows up at the same time. By the way, most concert-goers will not buy tickets in advance for general admission shows. Why should they, unless the show has potential to sell out. If you plan to attend a general admission show and have not purchased your tickets early, I would recommend that you purchase your ticket at least on the morning of the show and not wait until one hour prior to the show. You may get very annoyed at having to wait in long lines.

Festival Seating is a designated location where there are no chairs; in other words, standing room only. It has been my experience that this can be one of the most dangerous situations a concert-goer could allow himself or herself to get into. When you put an excessive amount of people into a limited amount of space, you create the formula for a Safety Hazard. Venue management must be very careful to avoid problems, but a good management team will have researched and anticipated problems. Just be aware so that you can help the venue keep everything safe and enjoyable. Cooperation makes everyone's concert better.

When caution is used, and the venue controls the numbers of people entering and leaving the space, the situation improves tremendously. There are other things, such as staff, barricades, signage, turnstiles, and wristbands that can be used to provide a safer environment for festival seating. Obviously, the control of these types of safety issues and concerns will vary from one venue to the next. Hopefully, it's not just the venue making these decisions. I would hope there are local venue codes and fire codes that would help to prevent unsafe conditions during concerts. It has been my experience that the local fire departments can be of great assistance for life safety issues.

SEATING ANALYSIS

Reserved Seating End Stage
Seating analysis will vary with each venue

Assumptions for this analysis are:
- 5,000-12,000 seats
- Floor area 20-25 thousand sf
- Ceiling Height 40-90 ft
- Stage Size 40'-60'

- Front Row – *Great, but not for everyone*
- 2nd to 10th Row – *The closer, the better*
- 11th row and back – *Hard to see over others, and people stand*
- Side of stage view – *May not see a lot of the show; Good view at times*
- Lower Level seating 1-2 rows above floor – *People walking block your view*
- End Risers – *O.K., if not too far from stage*
- Box Level Seating with a 30 to 45 degrees elevated view of stage – *Good*
- Close Box Level Seating with 30 to 45 degree elevation – *Excellent*
- Upper Level Seating first few rows – *may have sight-line problems*
- Upper Level Seating 50 yard line 4-20 rows up – *OK*
- Upper Level Seating 10-40 yard line 4-20 rows up – *OK*
- Upper Level Seating 20 rows and up – *Not so good to Fair*

All the above will vary accordingly for each venue.

The Do's and Don'ts

THE DO'S

Policies & Procedures are not the same at all venues.

- Most of the time, you can bring small cameras.
- Bring some extra film.
- Read the back of the ticket.
- Arrive early.
- Bring an umbrella if needed.
- Bring aspirin.
- Bring ear plugs.
- Bring some binoculars.
- Bring a small pocket flashlight.
- Prepare for room temperature change.
- If venue has hockey team and in-ice, seats on the floor may be cold.
- Bring a cellular phone (optional, but helpful).
- Bring a blanket for outdoor concerts.
- Bring a lawn chair for outdoor concerts.
- Bring cash; not all venues have teller machines.
- Check with venue to find out if large video screens will be used.

THE DON'TS

Policies & Procedures are not the same at all venues.

- Video cameras are not allowed in most cases.
- No alcoholic beverages.
- No glass containers.
- No firearms.
- No food items.
- No coolers (some exceptions with outdoor venues).
- No illegal drugs.
- No pets (exception: seeing-eye dogs).
- No skateboards.
- Don't stand in aisles.
- Don't run inside venue.
- Don't stand in seated areas (exception: first song & encore).
- Don't smoke in non-smoking area.
- Don't drink and drive.
- Don't stand in chairs.
- Don't lean on rails.
- Don't walk to your car alone.
- Don't buy counterfeit novelties.
- Don't knowingly sit in the wrong seats.

Special Programs and Services

The **Parent's Room** or **Quiet Room** is a designated area for you, the parent, and/or friend, to wait during the performance of a concert. This room may be set up with a few tables, some chairs, cards, games, soft drinks, etc. If you have a young child or teenager attending a concert, this may be a great place for you to wait for your child.

 Don't Drink and Drive Programs have become very popular for many venues across the country. Some venues refer to it as the **Designated Drivers Program**.

What this typically will do for you as a concert-goer is allow you to designate yourself as the designated driver, and, in return, you may receive a free soft drink or whatever the venue may be giving to the designated driver. To sign up for this program, you may be required to sign a designated driver's form and/or wear a designated driver's wristband or button. The designated drivers program is a very good program and tells me that the venue is a positive player. Also, a **Free Ride Home Program** is in place at most venues where alcoholic beverages are being served and a designated drivers program is in place.

Cellular Phone Service is becoming very popular for some venues. This is basically a customer service program. The one that I'm familiar with allows you, the concert-goer, to fill out a short form as you enter the venue. You then can use the phone for outgoing local calls, and you can also call home and leave a designated cellular phone number with someone, such as a baby sitter, to call in case of an emergency. At the cellular booth or table, you can leave your name and seat locations in case of an emergency phone call. In the event you had an emergency call, someone from the cellular booth would locate you and bring you a cellular phone to return the emergency call. This is an excellent customer service program.

Americans With Disabilities Act

Venues all across the country have dealt with the implementation of the **Americans with Disabilities Act**. Venues have found that more concert-goers with disabilities have now begun to attend more concerts. I think it's great that everyone now has the same opportunities to get out and attend these concerts. I served as chairman of a venue committee that was charged with identifying physical barriers for the disabled in our venue. We also identified solutions to those barriers. This was a great experience for me to have served on such a committee. One of my experiences involved spending several hours in a wheelchair at our venue myself. That experience gave me a whole new perspective of our venue. The following areas of general discussion are just a few I have chosen to comment on. I'm certainly not an expert in this area, and none of this will be referred to as code.

Parking is always a real concern for the disabled. Sometimes it is very difficult for a disabled person to travel a long distance. I would encourage anyone who has parking concerns to call the venue prior to arrival. It may be possible to park near the venue to accommodate such needs. A drop off area may also be a possibility for many people. Most venues are required to hold a percentage of parking spaces for the disabled. Please have disabled parking stickers properly displayed.

Wheelchair Seating is and should be available in all venues. Prior to purchasing tickets, please inform the ticket seller of your disability concerns. If you or whomever you are purchasing the ticket for has any type of disability, please inform the ticket-seller at the point of purchase. Most venues make provisions for all types of disabilities. It has been my experience that for each wheelchair ticket location there is one accompanist seat sold next to the wheelchair location. Wheelchairs may or may not be available at the venue, so I would recommend that you call the venue prior to arriving if you desire to use a wheelchair provided by the venue. Special seating is also held for the hearing impaired and the blind.

Do not hesitate to inform the venue if you have any concerns or special needs. **When Purchasing Tickets**, please be aware that most venues are required by law to provide a certain number of seats for the disabled. The following are a few examples of how the disabled seating may be handled at the box office.

- **Wheelchair Seating** and one accompanying person
- **Hearing Impaired** and one accompanying person
- **Sight Impaired** and one accompanying person

Again, there will be other type disabled seats available at each venue and I would encourage anyone with a disability concern to contact the venue for specific information.

Concessions

In most venues, **concessions** are a primary source of income. You will find typical items, such as soft drinks, french fries, pizza, beer, hot dogs, hamburgers, pickles, candy, and many specialty items. A recent survey showed the number-one product sold at concessions stands is the soft drink. As a concert-goer, I would look for the health department rating that should be posted inside the food area. If the venue has a good rating, I would evaluate the price of the product prior to placing the order. A good time to do this is by picking up a menu on the way in if one is available.

There are a few simple things that you, the concert-goer can do to help **avoid** those **long lines** that you typically run into at concert venues. If possible, purchase your tickets on the left-hand side of the venue. Since most of us are right-handed, we have this natural instinct to do everything to the right. The typical concert-goer will enter on the right-hand side of the venue and then want to turn right again. If you will think a little more to the left, you will usually find that lines on the left are shorter.

Another method for avoiding the long lines would be to select an aisle seat near the concession stand. An aisle seat allows for quick and easy access to the concession stand. The aisle seat also has a few other advantages that are discussed in other areas of this guide. Obviously, another way to avoid the long lines is to go to the concession stand during the performance. While you may miss one or two songs, it might still be worth it. I have seen people go out to the concession stands and wait fifteen to twenty minutes during the intermission and still miss a song or two.

If you're very lucky, you might be in a venue were they take orders, and you never have to leave your seat. Sounds great, doesn't it? I have read of a few venues that have such a system for professional sports, but I'm not familiar with one doing this successfully for concerts. I have heard of a few venues hawking a few food items during concerts.

Novelties are items such as shirts, jackets, hats, and photographs that are sold before, during, and after the concert. Novelties can be an excellent source of revenue for the artist and the venue. Approximately thirty to forty percent of the people attending a concert will spend some money on novelties. Most of the novelties sold at concerts are of good quality; however, in most cases, you will pay a premium price for these novelties. For many concert-goers, those $25 T-Shirts are not just a novelty item, but a souvenir and a special memory of the concert.

Don't Get Ripped Off by purchasing counterfeit merchandise outside the venue. Yes, there are people who manufacture counterfeit novelties and merchandise such as T-Shirts and hats. You can sometimes buy this merchandise in the parking areas near the venue. I have  seen a lot of this counterfeit merchandise, and I have never seen a quality product. On occasions, undercover police confiscate some of these shirts, and I have taken them home just to see how long they would last. I can honestly say they don't last very long, and I would encourage you not to purchase counterfeit merchandise.

The
Fan
Club

Ten years ago, I was observing four or five fan club members in the backstage area. The fan club members appeared to have it made. While everyone else was trying to talk their way backstage to meet their favorite entertainer, these people just remained cool, calm, and collected as they met their favorite entertainer. A few years passed, and these fan club memberships have grown from four or five to 10, then 20, then 50, and now in the thousands for some artists. If you want to increase your chances of meeting your favorite artist, I would encourage you to join his or her fan club. It's typically only a few dollars a year to join, and you get several other benefits, such as quarterly fan club mail and the privilege to purchase fan club concert tickets.

FAN CLUBS

Artist: **Alabama**
Address: Alabama Fan Club
P.O. Box 529
Ft. Payne, AL 35967

Artist: **Tim McGraw**
Address: International Fan Club
P.O. Box 128138
Nashville, TN 37212

Artist: **Garth Brooks**
Address: The Believer Magazine
P.O. Box 507
Goodlettsville, TN 37070-0507

Artist: **Sawyer Brown**
Address: Sawyer Brown Fan Club
4219 Hillsboro Road
Suite #318
Nashville, TN 37215

Artist: **Reba McEntire**
Address: International Fan Club
P.O. Box 121996
Nashville, TN 37212-1996

Artist: **Alan Jackson**
Address: Alan Jackson Fan Club
P.O. Box 121945
Nashville, TN 37212-1945

Artist: **Brooks & Dunn**
Address: Honky Tonk Fan Club
P.O. Box 120669
Nashville, TN 37212-0669

Artist: **Jimmy Buffett**
Address: Parrot Heads
4255 Nora Lane
Duluth, GA 30136

Artist: **Tracy Byrd**
Address: Tracy Byrd Fan Club
P.O. Box 7703
Beaumont, TX 77726-7703

Artist: **George Strait**
Address: George Strait Fan Club
P.O. Box 2119
Hendersonville, TN 37077

Artist: **Rod Stewart**
Address: Rod Stewart Fan Club
P.O. Box 475
Morden, Surrey
SM4 6AT England

Artist: **Lynyrd Skynyrd**
Address: Lynyrd Skynyrd Fan Club
P.O. Box 120855
Nashville, TN 37212

Artist: **Vince Gill**
Address: Vince Gill Fan Club
P.O. Box 1407
White House, TN 37188

Artist: **Boyz 11 Men**
Address: International Fan Club
P.O. Box 884448
San Francisco, CA 94188

Artist: **Beach Boys**
Address: Beach Boys Fan Club
P.O. Box 84282
Los Angeles, CA 90073

Artist: **Ronnie Milsap**
Address: Ronnie Milsap Fan Club
P.O. Box 121831
Nashville, TN 37212-1831

Artist: **Charlie Daniels**
Address: Charlie Daniels Band Volunteers
17060 Central Pike
Lebanon, TN 37090

Artist: **Travis Tritt**
Address: Travis Tritt Country Club
P.O. Box 440099
Kennesaw, GA 30144

Artist: **Michael Bolton**
Address: International Fan Club
Fan Emporium Inc.
P.O. Box 679
Branford, CT 06405

Artist: **Clay Walker**
Address: Clay Walker Fan Club
P.O. Box 1304
Nederland, TX 77627

Artist: **Diamond RIO**
Address: Diamond RIO Fan Club
P.O. Box 24586
Nashville, TN 37202

Artist: **Van Halen**
Address: The International
Van Halen Magazine
784 N. 114 Street, Suite 200
Omaha, NE 68154

Artist: **George Michael**
Address: Faithmail Fan Club
1079 ML Amsterdam
The Netherlands

Artist: **David Lee Murphey**
Address: David Lee Murphey Fan Club
P.O. Box 24333
Nashville, TN 37202

Artist: **Oak Ridge Boys**
Address: International Fan Club
329 Rockland Road.
Hendersonville, TN 37075

Artist: **Eddie Rabbitt**
Address: Eddie Rabbitt Fan Club
P.O. Box 35286
Cleveland, OH 44135

Artist: **The Rolling Stones**
Address: The Stones (Fanzine)
P.O. Box 155
Suisun City, CA 94585

Artist: **Shenandoah**
Address: Shenandoah Fan Club
P.O. Box 120086
Nashville, TN 37212-0086

Artist: **Ricky Van Shelton**
Address: Ricky Van Shelton Fan Club
P.O. Box 120548
Nashville, TN 37212-0548

Artist: **Randy Travis**
Address: Randy Travis Fan Club
P.O. Box 38
Ashland, City, TN 3701

I have listed a few of my favorite artists with fan club information; however, if you would like more information on fan clubs for your favorite artists, please call or write the National Association of Fan Clubs.

National Association of Fan Clubs
P.O. Box 7487
Burbank, California 91510 U.S.A.

Phone: (818) 763-3280
Fax: (818) 752-4848

Customer
Service

The **concert-goer is the customer** when attending concerts in any venue. You should be treated like a customer. You should feel welcome and greeted with hospitality. Unfortunately, this is not always the case. Remember, you are a ticket-holder, and, without you and your support, the venue, promoter, and artist would make less money. I can assure you that everybody wants to make as much money as possible. If you are not treated like a customer, and you are not happy with the service you are receiving, then I would request to speak with someone from management. If you are still dissatisfied, then I would request a refund. I can tell you that refunds are much easier to get the night of the show than the next day. If you have a problem, bring it to the attention of the venue management immediately. Please keep in mind that the majority of venues all across the country are operated primarily by a part time work force.

Space and Service are the only two things that a venue really has to offer you, the customer. Think about it, what else does a venue have to offer? The space should be clean and acceptable to you. I would hope that the venue has a mission statement that would be valuable to the customer. Service includes those things like friendly people, meeting your needs, surpassing your expectations, jobs well done, and positive attitudes.

Unfortunately, not all venue managers have a customer service attitude, and sometimes your concert experiences may not be as good.

HIGHLIGHTS

- Reserved seating is the most widely used method for selling seats to concert-goers.
- Arrive early for the best general admission seat locations.
- Concert goers should be aware of possible problems with festival seating.
- Consider seating analysis when purchasing tickets.
- Read the back of your concert ticket.
- Take advantage of special programs.

  Don't Drink and Drive

  Designated Drivers Program

  Free Ride Home

  Free Cellular Phone Use
- Call the venue with any disability concerns.
- When possible, utilize the left hand side of the venue for faster service.
- Don't purchase counterfeit novelties.
- Fan club memberships are an excellent way of staying in touch with the concert environment.
- For fan club information, call the National Association of Fan Clubs (818) 763-3280.
- The ticket holder is the customer.

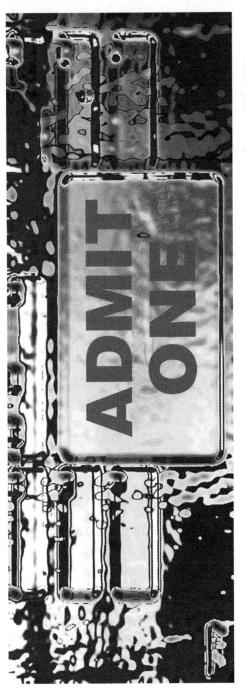

Is It
Really
Safe?

Crowd Control is one of many very important ingredients that go into the mix of having a successful concert. If all of the concert-goers had a great time and felt they'd gotten their money's worth, the venue, promoter, and artist felt the show was a success. If no one was injured and everyone made it home safely, it could be called an ideal concert. The question of safety will vary from one venue to the next and will depend a great deal on how much caution you take.

Festival Seating can be difficult if not properly controlled. Ask what measures the venue has taken and cooperate. Look for turnstiles, security, and wristbands for good general crowd control procedures in this area. If you are going to enter this area, I would look around and become familiar with all the exits in the designated area. Be careful, and use common sense, and you'll be much safer and happier.

Moshing is when a group of concert-goers get together and somewhat run into one another. When you see this for the first time, you might think that a fight is breaking out. The area designated for this is called a mosh pit. If there is not a designated area, the concert-goers will sometimes form an area to mosh in. Typically, the moshing area is located on the floor directly in front of the stage. Furthermore, body surfing and stage diving have become quite popular with some of the bands. Body surfing is when you are picked up and allow yourself to be passed around the crowd. If you are body surfing, then you keep your body tense and as straight as possible while other concert-goers pass you through the air. Some venues allow a body surfer to cross the barricade once or twice, but if you continue, you may be evicted. Stage Diving is the act of making your way to the stage, and then jumping off head first directly into the crowd. I like to see concert-goers have fun, but this is crazy. I have heard of some very serious injuries as a result of stage diving.

Exterior Lighting is extremely important, and I would like to see venues put more emphasis on the exterior lighting. At some concerts, there is more trouble outside the venue than inside the venue. Don't park in dark areas, and certainly don't walk alone in dark areas.

Adequate and Well-Trained Staffing can be the difference when it comes to having fun in a safe concert environment. A sufficient number of ticket-takers can get you into the venue faster and more safely. A sufficient number of ushers can help you find your seat quicker and more safely. A sufficient number of security and medical attendants is extremely important. If the venue cannot provide adequate and well-trained public service employees, then you are not in a safe environment. If *you* cannot identify several staff workers, then you should be concerned. Most venues, however, are careful to hire and train their staff.

Noise Levels should be taken into consideration by all concert-goers when attending concerts. It has been my experience that the heavy metal rock n'roll bands and the alternative bands are the loudest. Some of the country music bands are also generating a tremendous amount of decibels. I don't think this is a real problem for most concert-goers, because most of you will not be directly in front of the speakers for three hours straight. On occasion, you might find that the venue will provide you with ear plugs; however, I would encourage you to bring some ear plugs with you. I think that your hearing is one of those things that will catch up with you as you get older. My primary concern here would be for those concert-goers who stand directly in front of the speakers for several hours.

Alcoholic
Beverages

When attending concerts, you will find that some venues sell alcoholic beverages, and some venues don't. There are reasons for this, such as local laws and venue policies. The **Rules and Regulations** of these venues will vary from one extreme to the other. Some venues will sell you an alcoholic beverage as long as you can come up with the money. I really hate to say that, but it's true. I'm sure some of you may be thinking, "well, what's wrong with that? I'm an adult, and if I want another drink, then that's my business." To a certain extent, that is true. However, it should be and is the responsibility of the venue to insure the safety of *all* concert-goers.

When you look at it from that perspective, you can understand why most venues have controls on alcoholic beverages to help insure the safety of all concert-goers. Sometimes, we concert-goers are having so much fun that we don't even realize how much alcohol we have consumed; and, therefore, a concert-goer may have to be cut off by the bartender. Don't give the bartender a hard time; he or she is just doing his or her job. A venue with a well-trained staff will cut you off before you become overly intoxicated. There are several control mechanisms that some venues use to help insure the safety of everyone. The **Number of Alcoholic Beverages** that can be purchased by a concert-goer is one way of controlling consumption. I know that some venues will only sell two drinks at a time per person. So if you want more than that, you will have to get back in line to order again. Prior to purchasing drinks, some venues require that you go to the **Wristband** table to obtain a wristband. To get the wristband put onto your wrist, you will have to show legal identification that you are of age to consume alcoholic beverages. This wristband lets the servers know that you have already been properly checked and verified to be of the legal drinking age. I know some of you have experienced this process before and may or may not like it, but it's another excellent control mechanism.

For those of you who do not consume alcoholic beverages, then you may want to inquire about a possible **Non-Drinking Section**. I don't think the non-drinking section is very popular in the concert industry, and I would be surprised if very many venues even offer a non-drinking section. I think you will find the non-drinking section to be more suited for sporting events where you have a family environment.

The Internet

The **Internet** is changing the world in which we live. As a concert-goer, you now have more information available to you than ever before. If you enjoy concerts and would like to know more about your favorite entertainer, you need access to the Internet. You will find that some artists have set up their own homepage that will provide you with a variety of information. You can find tour dates, new music release dates, and fan club information for your favorite artist. You can also search for specific venues and find out who is scheduled for that venue. Several venues are setting up home pages so that you can access concert information for a specific event. You can find out some of the basic polices and procedures for a specific venue or event and learn ticket prices, as well as many other things that relate to a specific concert. It's a great way of communicating with the concert-goers. If you have not explored this information on the Internet, I would strongly encourage you to do so. You will find a great deal of this information by searching on **Arenas, Concerts, TicketMaster,** and **Pollstar**.

This is just the beginning of what concert-goers are going to be doing on the Internet. It's exciting, so start exploring the Internet, and I promise you that you will enhance your concert experience.

Concert
Promoters

A **Concert Promoter** is the person and/or company that has contracted with an artist, typically through an agency, for a specific date or dates. The promoter contracts a date with the venue for which the artist is to perform a concert and becomes the **risk taker**. Usually, the promoter will buy the show from the agency. For practical purposes and discussion, let's say the promoter pays the agency fifty percent of the money for the artist at the time the contract is signed. The remaining fifty percent will be paid on the day of the concert. Obviously, these agreements will vary accordingly and may have guarantees as well as percentages of the gross. I have heard of all kind of crazy deals made with promoters. Keep in mind that the promoter has usually invested several thousand dollars at this point and has absolutely no guarantee that the act will sell enough tickets to get any of his money back. On top of that, the promoter will contract with a venue to provide the necessary services to have such a concert. The promoter will typically pay the artist, venue rent, advertising, stagehands, catering, security, taxes, box office fees, staging, forklifts, and other miscellaneous expenses. Are you starting to see why promoters are the risk takers? If there is not enough ticket revenue to pay for all these expenses, guess who has to come up with the additional money to pay all the bills.

Venue Co-Promotions exist when a venue partners with a promoter to share some of the financial risk with the show. Usually, when a venue does this, the venue is putting more of its guaranteed dollars at risk. The upside is the opportunity to make more money if the concert does well. This method of promoting concerts has some risk; however, sometimes that is what it takes to make it happen. I'm certain that if some venues did not co-promote, they would not have as many concerts. Some venues, however, will not co-promote under any circumstances.

Booking Concerts

THE BASIC CONCEPT

The venue will ordinarily work with a concert promoter in an effort to bring concerts to your town. However, in some cases a venue will buy the show directly from the booking agency. The venue Manager, Assistant Manager, or the Marketing/Booking Sales Representative will typically try to book or negotiate for concerts with the promoter and/or the booking agency. Currently, booking concerts is a problem for many venues because there are just not that many acts on tour to support all the markets. Furthermore, many artists and bands are very expensive to book. There are a lot of costs associated with bringing good quality concerts to venues.

Once the concert is booked and all negotiations have been finalized, a written contract will be done. A file is created, and any information pertaining to the concert will be filed accordingly. A very important document that will need to go into this file is the insurance carrier information. It has been my experience that promoters will usually be required to provide the liability insurance for concerts. The venue will assign an event coordinator to work out the details of the event. The on-sale date will be determined and the process to set up tickets will begin. Shortly thereafter, a marketing strategy and advertising campaign will be implemented. The concert is set, the advertising is in place, and the lines for tickets have begun to form. At least, that's always the wish of all parties involved, but not necessarily the case. In this business, you just never know how a show is going to sell until the tickets have been sold.

The Book is actually the book that concert information is first entered into. The master book is used to record the date of the concert, the artist's name, and the promoter's name and phone number. It's really a simple process, until you have more than one promoter wanting the same dates or you start having to move dates in order to make concerts happen. This book may be one of the most important documents in the venue.

Several venues have **computerized their booking system**. The computerized booking system allows for much more flexibility. You can enter the necessary information very quickly. Once you enter the data, it is much easier to edit that data as needed. Report information is more readily available than ever before.

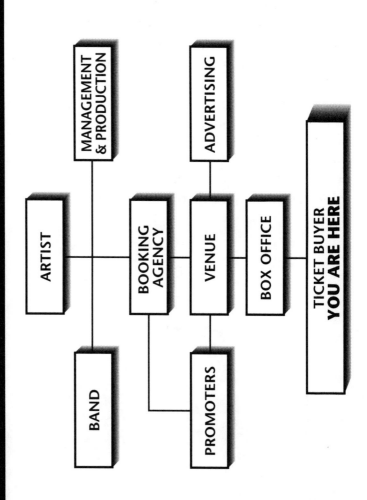

TYPICAL CONCERT FLOW CHART

MANAGEMENT & PRODUCTION

ADVERTISING

ARTIST

BOOKING AGENCY

VENUE

BOX OFFICE

TICKET BUYER
YOU ARE HERE

BAND

PROMOTERS

How
Venues
Make
Their
Money

Parking can be a great source of revenue for venues. Parking may be free at some venues; however, I can assure you that those lost revenues are being made up somewhere. The cost of parking will usually range anywhere from two dollars to five dollars depending on what part of the country you are located. I have heard of parking fees as high as ten dollars in some places. I would encourage you to spend your money wisely when it comes to parking. That extra couple of dollars may be worth it if you are getting secure and safe parking.

Concessions are a primary source of income, and venues will get deep into your pockets if you're not careful. When ordering, be specific as to the size of the product you are ordering. If you just order a soft drink, you may get one of those extra large drinks that requires both hands to carry at a cost of a few dollars. You definitely want to look at value pricing and get the best of the bad deals. Again, not all venues try to make all their money at the concession stand. Prices should be posted; if not, be sure to check prior to ordering.

The **Percentage of Gross Sales After Taxes** is a typical rent deal in the concert business. While there are many different types of rent deals, this one is often used against some form of guarantee or basic rent structure.

Flat Rental Fees are sometimes used in our industry; however, they are not very popular in today's market. Concerts have continued to grow at a rapid pace, and promoters and venues are finding it more and more difficult to make money. The artist's expenses have increased with the larger show, and, therefore, the artist are wanting more money. The bottom line is that you, the concert-goer, pay more for the tickets. Some artists have worked very hard to keep ticket prices down, and that's very encouraging.

Novelties are an excellent revenue source for the artist and the venue. For some reason, I'm leaving the promoter out, and that just doesn't seem right. I'm sure they get their share somehow. On a good night and with a hot selling artist, thousands of shirts and other novelty items are sold. This translates into thousands and thousands of dollars. Think about it; each person attending the concert could spend an average of five to ten dollars purchasing novelty items. A word of caution: don't get caught up in trying to save a few dollars and purchase a cheaper T-shirt from a scalper. They're out there counterfeiting those shirts at a cheap price because that's exactly what they are – "cheap." Most of those counterfeited shirts that you might buy outside the venue on some street corner won't last a few weeks or one washing. **Buyer beware of counterfeit shirts.**

Staffing and Equipment are typical areas of income for venues. Venues will rent out labor as a profit center. Such labor includes security, ticket takers, ticket sellers, ushers, electricians, stagehands, runners, etc. The venue will also rent equipment such as staging, tables, chairs, spotlights, etc.

Computerized Ticketing is an excellent way for venues to make money. If they own their own computerized ticketing system, they can charge a ticket surplus charge and/or handling charge that remains with the venue. I don't know of too many venues that are doing this, because it can be a real headache of a problem. Most venues contract for a computerized ticketing service, but still make a small percentage of revenue.

The **Box Office** can also be a revenue producer for venues. Venues often get a percentage of tickets sales to cover expenses at the box office. I'm sure there is a little revenue built into that. Some venues charge promoters for a box office set-up fee for selling tickets. Most promoters hate to pay for a ticket set-up fee.

Credit Cards are probably a very small source of income for most venues. It might even be an expense for some venues. The idea here is that the venue will typically charge the concert-goer or promoter more to use the credit card than the venue is having to pay. Most concert-goers are still paying cash, but the trend for credit card users has definitely increased over the years.

Surcharges from the Venue are additional charges added to the price of the ticket that go directly to the venue. This may be called a seating tax, a capital improvement tax, venue tax, venue maintenance tax, or, in some cases, just a ticket surcharge. I'm sure there are many different methods for identifying this surcharge. Basically, it's an easy way for a venue to increase revenues at the expense of the ticket buyers. If you are being charged this tax, then I would certainly expect the venue to be very clean and well-maintained. If you are going to pay a reasonably high price for a concert ticket, then you should expect some quality in return.

HIGHLIGHTS

- Be extremely careful when participating in moshing activities.
- Avoid walking alone when possible, especially in parking areas.
- Bring ear plugs for hearing protection when applicable.
- Wristbands for purchasing alcoholic beverages is an excellent control mechanism for venues.
- Some venues offer a non-drinking section. (Alcoholic Beverage)
- The Internet is an excellent tool for concert information.
- The promoter is the risk-taker.
- Parking can be a great source of income for venues.
- Concessions maybe the largest form of revenue generated by a venue.
- Rental arrangements for most venues are negotiable and flexible.

Conclusion

In the introduction, I told you the concert environment is extremely unique and has many interesting attributes. I hope that by now you, too, agree that the concert environment is indeed unique and interesting. From a concert-goer's perspective, you now have a better understanding of a venue and what to do to get to know a venue even better. The venue is an integral part of the concert experience. When you can become comfortable with the venue, you will have a better concert experience, and the way to become comfortable with a venue is to have an understanding of its purpose and how it functions. Event awareness consist of several vehicles of communications to you as a concert-goer and is a very important part of the concert environment when planning your concert. Be sure to take advantage of any free form of advertisements made available to you. Many venues will be glad to add your name to the mailing list at no cost to you. If you are aware of the concert and the on-sale date, then you are one step ahead of many concert-goers. The box office is the one area of the concert environment that most concert-goers are already familiar with; however, be sure to reference the top 10 criteria I have provided for you on page 43. Have your seating chart with you when making your seat selection; it is important that you know what the best seats are. Sometimes a good way to purchase good tickets is through group sales. If you are going to consider group sales, call the venue prior to the event going on sale.

Computerized ticketing is more often the very best way for a venue to sell tickets. It's fair, convenient, and offers equal access to all concert-goers. Computerized ticketing is also in the best interest of the concert-goer in most cases. Simply put, the ticket outlet that does the least amount of business will most likely be the best location for purchasing the best seats. Be sure to check with the venue for special programs and services. Many of these programs and services are not taken advantage of.

Fan Clubs continue growing in popularity, and if you really want to stay in touch with a particular artist or band, then I would consider joining the fan club. This is an excellent way to increase your chances of meeting your favorite artists.

The Internet is also an excellent tool for concert information. You can find tour dates, ticket prices, artists home pages, and much more with just a few simple key strokes. It is a wonderful way to stay informed.

Any time an immense number of people attend a concert or any other event for that matter, certain crowd management procedures are required for a safer environment. Thanks to many well trained venue Managers, venue staff, and organizations such as International Association of Auditorium Managers (IAAM), concert-goers are much safer when attending concerts and will have much more fun.

Glossary

Advance Deposit - Partial payment to hold a specific date. A partial payment when contracting an artist to perform.

Advertising - A process of informing ticket buyers about concerts.

Against a Percentage - A percentage of gross vs. a flat cost.

Agent - A person or company who represents business contracts for an artist.

Allocation - A process of releasing a specific number of tickets to other parties involved in ticket sales.

Amphitheater - An outdoor facility that is capable of hosting concerts. The seating area is generally a semicircular shape, fitting to the surrounding landscape.

Amplification - Increase in signal of power level.

Arena - A facility designed for large crowds to attend sporting events, concerts, and other events as deemed appropriate. Typically, there is a main, flat floor and fixed seating that surrounds the floor and rises to different levels.

Audit Stub - A small part of the ticket to be torn and used by the box office for accounting functions.

Available Dates - Dates available for bookings.

Backstage Pass - A pass for gaining access to the backstage area.

Barricade - A structure designed to obstruct and direct movement of a crowd.

Block Seating - Seats held close together for group sales or sponsors.

Booking - The process of contracting for a specific date or dates.

Box Office - The designated location in or near the building where a concert-goer can purchase tickets.

Building Diagrams - A graphic drawing showing the basic layout of the building. A typical building diagram will show parking, entrances, exits, phones, and restrooms.

Building Manager - The staff person directly responsible for the day to day operation of the building.

Building Staff - The employees working for the building.

Buying a Show - The process of committing on a firm basis to promote an artist.

Capacity - The total number of patrons permitted for a specific event.

Cap - A not to exceed dollar amount.

Clean - A sold out performance.

Club Seating - A special seating arrangement for the right of first refusal to purchase a specific seat.

Coliseum - A large facility primarily designated for sporting events. See Arena

Comps - Free tickets

Computer Tickets - Tickets printed for a specific event.

Computerized Ticketing - Tickets equally distributed via ticket outlets.

Concert Agenda - The time intervals of the concert.

Continental Seating - Seating with wider spacing between rows and no aisles running toward the stage.

Co-Promotion - When two or more parties are participating in an event for a profit and/or loss. All parties may not share the same profits or risk.

Crowd Control - The management of direction and demeanor of an audience.

Curtain Time - The time at which the performance begins.

Customer Convenience Fee - A fee added to the price of the ticket for the convenience of purchasing the ticket. (Normally not added when tickets are purchased at the building.)

Dark Days - No activity in the facility.

Deadwood - Unsold tickets

Dimmer - A piece of equipment used to dim stage or house lights.

Direct-Dialing - The direct-line phone number.

Direct Mail - A form of promotion in which material is mailed directly to a potential buyer.

Downstage - The front of the stage closest to the audience.

Dressing The House - Spreading the tickets out to give the event a better look.

Dumping - The process of adding unclaimed seats to the system.

Dupes - Duplicate tickets

Entertainer's Staff - Employees of the artists or band.

Event Day - The day for which the event is taking place.

Event Guide - Information about events.

Event Security - Security that is assigned to the event.

Event Settlement - The financial process for determining profits or loss of a concert.

Exhibition Hall - Large room with flat floor space. Primarily used for exhibitions and meetings. Some smaller concerts are held in exhibition halls.

Festival Seating - A form of general admission (No Seating Available). Patrons are expected to stand.

Front Act - The artists or band designated to open the show. (Opening Act)

Front Money - Money required in advance of a concert.

General Admission - Open seating on a first come first served basis.

Grass Seats - A designated seating area where no seats will be provided. (The patron is expected to bring seating or stand.)

Group Sales - Tickets ordered by a group, normally required to order a minimum number of tickets.

Hard Tickets - Pre-printed tickets ordered by the box office.

Holds - Tickets held prior to going on sale.

Information Packets - Information about the venue.

Internet - The World Wide Web of computer-generated information. The process of sharing and advertising information via a world wide computer network.

Kiosks - A free standing structure primarily used for advertisement and ticket sales.

Lap Seat - A discounted ticket price for a child who will not occupy a seat.

Lost & Found - A designated area for items to be stored until properly identified by owner.

Management Fee - A fee for performing some service for the venue, such as a food and beverage contract with a private company.

Manifest - An inventory of the number of tickets with price per ticket.

Marketing - A process of planning and promoting an event.

Marquee - An outdoor display used for advertisements.

Media - Methods through which a message is communicated to the public.

Metal Detector - A device used for detecting metals.

Minimum - A guaranteed minimum of payment for the use of space.

Mission Statement - A brief statement for which the organization was created and/or a brief statement indicating goals and purpose.

Multipurpose Center - A venue that is equipped to allow multiple types of usage.

Moshing - A combination of slam dancing, body surfing, head banging and stage diving. The area in which moshing takes place is known as the moshing pit.

Net - Remaining monies after all expenses have been paid.

Novelties - Items such as T-shirts, hats and photographs of artists.

Off The Top - Monies paid out prior to expenses.

Open Doors - The time in which patrons can enter the venue.

Paper The House - A process of giving out free tickets in an effort to fill the house.

Parents Room - A designated waiting room for non ticket holders.

Pat Downs - A light search for unauthorized items not permitted inside the venue.

Patron - A person attending the concert.

Pencil In - A temporary hold on a booking.

Press Release - A newsworthy occurrence usually intended to promote an event.

Promoter - The person or company responsible for all cost associated with an event.

Promotion - Marketing activities to increase event awareness.

Reserved Seating - A seat reserved for a specific ticket holder.

Rigger - A person who installs the rigging system hardware.

Road Crew - The people who travel with the production.

Runner - A person hired to go for items needed on the day of the show.

Scalped Ticket - A ticket sold at a cost higher than face value.

Seating Chart - A graphic display of a venue used for selecting seats.

Smoking Policies - Venue policies for smokers and non smokers, Designated smoking areas when applicable.

Snake - Multiple conductor cable often used for connecting sound and lighting equipment.

Standing Room Only - Tickets sold on the basis of standing only.

Sponsorships - Typically large companies underwriting all or part of the cost associated with a specific event.

Stage Hand - Personnel working with the production of the concert.

Stage Manager - The person in charge of the concert production once the performance has begun.

Stage Left - The left side of the stage as one faces the audience from the stage.

Stage Right - The right side of the stage as one faces the audience from the stage.

Ticket - Printed voucher for obtaining access to a specific event.

Ticket Outlet - A designated location for ticket buyers to purchase tickets.

Ticket Scalper - A person selling tickets for a profit.

Ticket Taker - A person responsible for taking tickets.

Turnstile Count - The number of patrons passing through a turnstile.

Upstage - The part of the stage that is farthest from the audience.

Usher - A person responsible for seating patrons.

Venue - A specific building or facility where concerts are held.

Walk-Ups - Day of show ticket sales.

Wheelchair Seats - Designated seating to accommodate wheelchairs.

Will Call - Tickets that have been set aside for pick up..

Will Call Window - The designated window or designated location for will call tickets to be picked up.

Wristbands - A plastic band affixed to the wrist for some form of identification.

References:
International Association of Auditorium Managers (IAAM)
Webster's Dictionary

Index